HAPPY EASTER

D1432944

I SPY with my little eye something starting with...

A is for Aerostat

I SPY with my little eye something starting with...

B is for Bunny

I SPY with my little eye something starting with...

C is for Cake

I SPY with my little eye something starting with...

D is for Dog

I SPY with my little eye something starting with...

E is for Eggs

I SPY with my little eye something starting with...

F is for Flowers

I SPY with my little eye something starting with...

G is for Gift

I SPY with my little eye something starting with...

H is for Hat

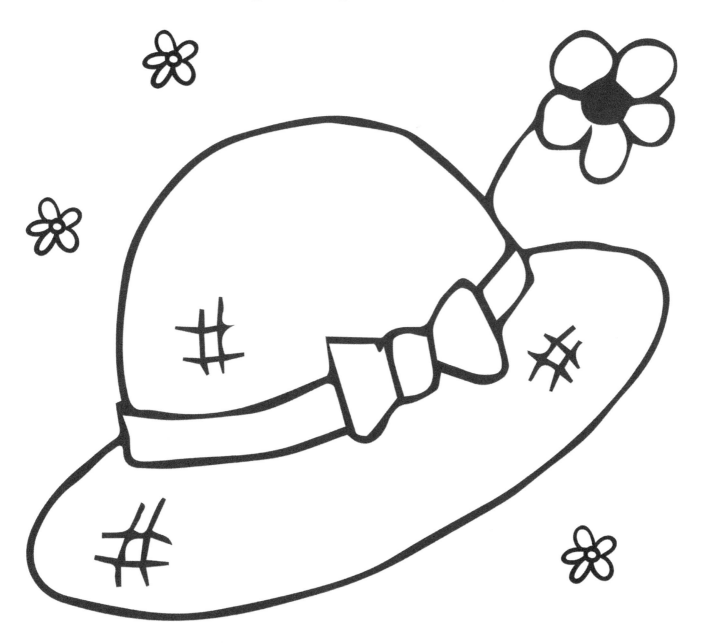

I SPY with my little eye something starting with...

I is for Ice cream

I SPY with my little eye something starting with...

J is for Jellyfish

I SPY with my little eye something starting with...

K is for Key

I SPY with my little eye something starting with...

L is for Ladybug

I SPY with my little eye something starting with...

M is for Mouse

I SPY with my little eye something starting with...

N is for Nest

I SPY with my little eye something starting with...

O is for Owl

I SPY with my little eye something starting with...

P is for Pig

I SPY with my little eye something starting with...

Q is for Queen

I SPY with my little eye something starting with...

R is for Rainbow

I SPY with my little eye something starting with...

S is for Sun

I SPY with my little eye something starting with...

T is for Trumpet

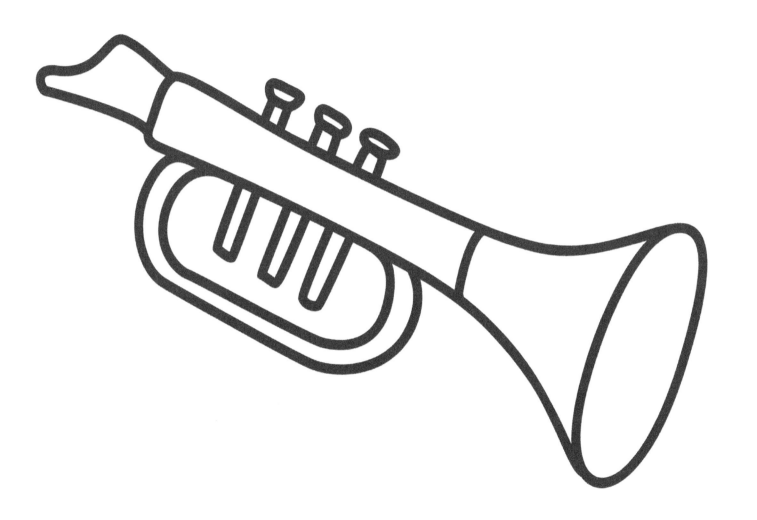

I SPY with my little eye something starting with...

U is for Unicorn

I SPY with my little eye something starting with...

V is for Vase

I SPY with my little eye something starting with...

W is for Worm

I SPY with my little eye something starting with...

X is for Xylophone

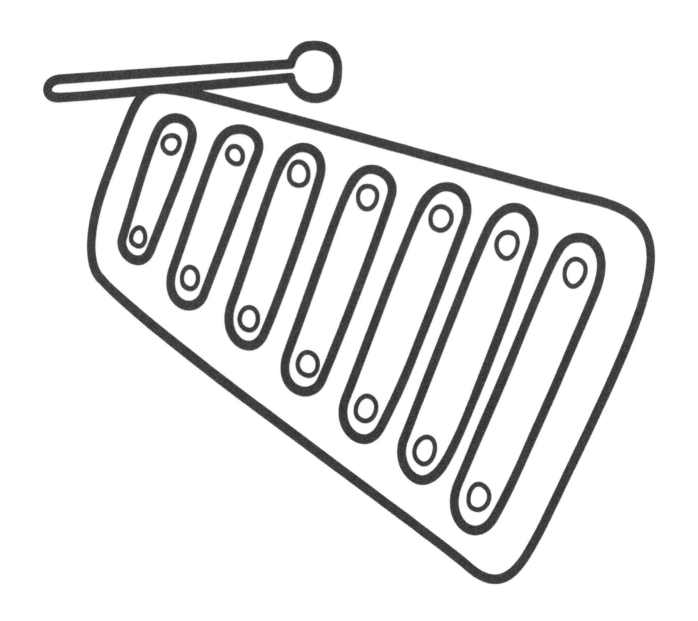

I SPY with my little eye something starting with...

Y is for Yacht

I SPY with my little eye something starting with...

Z is for Zebra

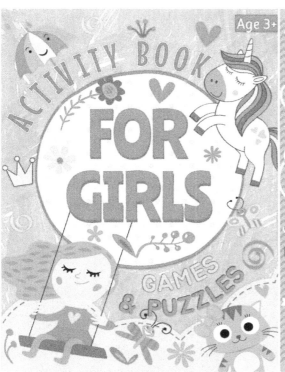

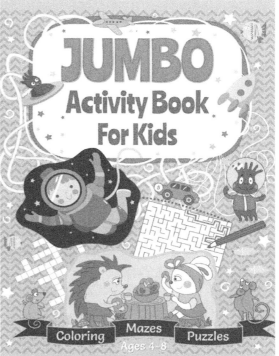

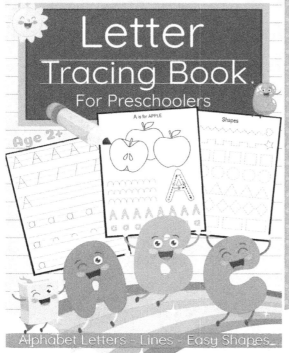

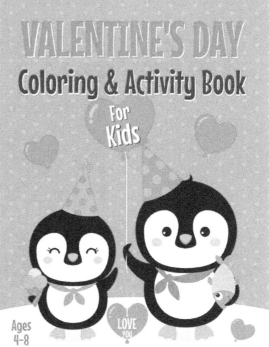

Mew Press

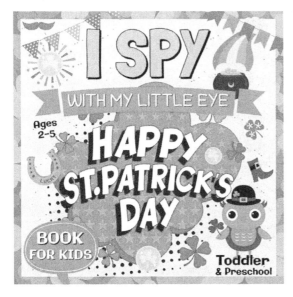

Made in the USA
Monee, IL
28 March 2021